MATH RIDDLES
FOR SMART KIDS

MATH RIDDLES AND BRAIN TEASERS
THAT KIDS AND FAMILIES WILL LOVE

M. PREFONTAINE

CONTENTS

Introduction

"The mind once stretched by a new idea, never returns to its original dimensions."

Ralph Waldo Emerson

This collection of 150 brain teasing math riddles and puzzles is the third in a series of riddles books. Their purpose is to make children think out of the box and stretch the mind. Created to test logic, lateral thinking as well as memory and to engage the brain in seeing patterns and connections between different things and circumstances, this book will be an interesting companion for many hours.

These are more difficult riddles and are designed to be attempted by children from 10 years onwards, as well as participation from the rest of the family.

They are laid out in three chapters which get more difficult as you go through the book, in the author's opinion at least. The answers are at the back of the book if all else fails.

Have fun!

DIFFICULT RIDDLES

1. Two fathers and two sons sat down to eat eggs for breakfast. They ate exactly three eggs; each person had an egg. How was this?

2. Find the number that completes the following sequence:
   1   4   9   16   ?   36   49

3. Which set of numbers would most logically come next in the following sequence?
   10   1   9   2   8   3   7   4   6   5   5
   6   4   7   3   8   2   ?

4. Divide 110 into two parts so that one will be 150 percent of the other. What are the two numbers?

5. How many times can you subtract the number 5 from 25?

6. I am a three-digit number. My tens digit is five more than my ones digit. My hundreds digit is eight less than my tens digit. What number am I?

7. Which 3 numbers have the same answer whether they're added or multiplied together?

8. There is a basket containing 5 apples. How do you divide the apples among 5 children so that each child has 1 apple while 1 apple remains in the basket?

9. The beach resort held a contest to guess the number of beach balls in the net bag. Pearl guessed 20, Alex guessed 21, James guessed 22, Dick guessed 17 and Adam guessed 16. One was off by 4, one was off by 3, one by 1, one by 2 and one was correct. How many beach balls were there?

10. Mr. Jones has 2 children. If the older child is a boy, what is the probability that the younger child is a boy, too?

11. John has been hired to paint the numbers 1 through 100 on 100 apartments. How many times will he paint the number 8?

12. What is 40 divided by 1/2, plus 15?

13. Two boys, John and Peter, are running a 100-meter race. In the first race that they run John beats Peter by 5 meters. To make things fair, the next time they race John stands 5 meters behind the starting line. If they run at the same speed as the first race who will win the second race?

14. A man goes into a barber shop and gets a $15 haircut. He pays the barber with a $20 bill, but the barber doesn't have change because it is an especially slow day. The barber goes to the flower shop next to his own and trades the $20 bill for one $10 dollar bill and two $5 bills. Then he gives the man his $5 in change. Later, the lady from the flower shop confronts the barber and tells him that the $20 bill he gave her was counterfeit. The barber agrees and he gives the lady a different $20 bill. Later that day he tries to figure out how much money he lost. What did he lose?

15. There are two planes. One is going from New York to London at a speed of 600 MPH. The other is traveling from London to New York at a speed of 500 MPH. When the planes meet which one will be closer to London?

16. If you have two twins, three triplets and four quadruplets, how many people do you have?

17. A teacher of mathematics used an unconventional method to measure a 15-minute time limit for a test. He just used 7- and 11-minute hourglasses. During the whole time he turned hourglasses only 3 times (turning both hourglasses at once counts as one flip). Explain how the teacher measured 15 minutes.

18. What mathematical symbol can be placed between 5 and 9 to get a number greater than 5 and smaller than 9?

19. What is the 4-digit number (no zeros) in which the first and last digits are the same, the second digit is half the sum of the second and the fourth, and the last digit is half the sum of the first and third? (The sum of all digits is 24.)

20. What number comes next in the sequence? 1, 6, 13, 22, 33, ?

21. The math department was planning for a farewell luncheon to honor one of their retiring colleagues. They calculated that it would cost each person $30. "It's lucky that there aren't five fewer of us to split the bill, or it would be $10 more each", said one of the math teachers. How many people would be splitting the bill, and how much did the luncheon cost?

22. What 3-digit number (including a decimal point) will give you the same answer whether you subtract 5 or divide by 5?

23. If 6 puzzle solvers can solve 12 puzzles in 12 minutes, how long should it take a single puzzle solver to solve 60 puzzles?

24. There are 2 numbers that total 225 and have a ratio of 2 to 13. What are the numbers?

25. What is the 4-digit number (no zeros) in which the third and fourth digits are a baker's dozen; the second digit is the sum of the third and fourth, and the first digit is double the last?

26. How long is a rope that is 2 yards shorter than another rope that is three times the length of the first rope?

27. What is the number which is 5 more than one fifth of one tenth of one fourth of 1,000?

28. What number gives the same result when it is added to 1 ½ and when it is multiplied by 1 ½?

29. What 2 numbers will give you an answer of 36 when the smaller is subtracted from the larger and an answer of 1,440 when one is multiplied by the other?

30. Five soccer teams were competing in a tournament where they face each other exactly once. After the tournament, the following is the point table where teams get 2 points for a win and 1 for a draw:
Manchester Utd 6
Barcelona 5
Bayern 4
Milan 2
Real Madrid?
How many points did Real Madrid end up with?

31. At a fruit stand, an orange costs 18¢, a pineapple costs 27¢, and a grape costs 15¢. Using the same logic, can you tell how much a mango costs?

32. Can you find four consecutive prime numbers that add up to 220?

33. A large number of people went to a party and they decided to make some fun at the bar:
The first person asks the barman for half a pint of beer.
The second person asks for a quarter pint of beer.
The third person asks for one-eighth of beer and so on ...
How many pints of beer will the barman need to fulfill the beers ordered?

34. Fill in the missing numbers in the following series:
101   99   102   98   103   97   ?   ?

35. Jack flew to Australia at the fantastic speed of 1,000 miles per hour. There he picked up his friend and flew back, burdened by the extra weight, at only 500 miles per hour. What was his average speed?

36. Which number when added to 5/4 gives the same result as when it is multiplied 5/4?

37. Annette took an exam that had 20 questions. The total grade was calculated by awarding 10 points for each correct answer and deducting 5 points for each incorrect answer. Annette answered all 20 questions and received a score of 125. How many wrong answers did she have?

38. There are several chickens and rabbits in a cage (with no other types of animals). There are 72 heads and 200 feet inside the cage. How many chickens are there, and how many rabbits?

39. A recycling factory makes its own paper cups for canteen use. It can make one new cup from nine used ones. If it has 515 used cups how many can it possibly make in total?

40. If it takes 6 florist's assistants 3 hours to pack 12 boxes of flowers, how fast can sixteen assistants pack 16 boxes?

41. Two slow moving trains are traveling towards each other. One train runs from point A to point B at 19 miles an hour. The other train runs from point B to point A at 21 miles per hour. One hour before the trains pass each other, how far apart are they?

42. When asked how old he was, Bob replied, "In 2 years I will be twice as old as I was five years ago." How old is he?

43. 4 fathers, 2 grand-fathers and 4 sons went to watch a movie. What is the minimum number of the tickets they need to buy?

44. If you reverse the digits of Jane's age, you will have the age of her grandmother. Her grandmother's age is also the sum of the two digits of Jane's age squared. What are their ages?

45. If a family has four children, what is the probability that all four are the same sex?

46. If 5 cats can catch 5 mice in 5 minutes, how many cats do you need to catch 100 mice in 100 minutes?

47. In a stable there are men and horses. In all, there are 22 heads and 72 feet. How many men and how many horses are in the stable?

48. A mile-long train is moving at 60 miles per hour when it reaches a mile-long tunnel. How long does it take the entire train to pass through the tunnel?

49. A half is a third of it. What is it?

50. A farmer came to town with some watermelons. He sold half of them plus half a melon, and found that he had one whole melon left. How many melons did he take to town?

51. There are a mix of red, green and blue balls in a bag. The total number of balls is 60. There are four times as many red balls as green balls and 6 more blue balls than green balls. How many balls of each color are there?

52. John bought a bag of oranges on Monday, and ate a third of them. On Tuesday, he ate half of the remaining oranges. On Wednesday, he looked in the bag to find that he only had two oranges left. How many oranges were originally in the bag?

53. Sally is 54 years old and her mother is 80. How many years ago was Sally's mother three times her age?

54. You have a glass of water that looks about half full. How can you tell, only using the glass of water itself, if the glass is half full or not? The glass is a right cylinder.

55. A ship anchored in a port has a ladder which hangs over the side. The length of the ladder is 200 cm, the distance between each rung is 20 cm and the bottom rung touches the water. The tide rises at a rate of 10 cm an hour. When will the water reach the fifth rung?

56. What number do you get when you multiply all of the numbers on a telephone's number pad?

57. There are several books on a bookshelf. If one book is the 4th from the left and 6th from the right, how many books are on the shelf?

58. What's the angle between minute hand and hour hand at a quarter past three?

59. There are two ropes that both take exactly 1 hour to burn from end to end. You are unable to cut the rope. How can you burn the two ropes in a total of exactly 45 minutes?

60. James is buying some new fishing equipment at a sporting goods store where there is a sale. Everything in the store is 25% off, and cash purchases receive another 25% off the sale price. What will James pay in cash for the fishing equipment with a pre-sale price of $100?

61. If you have a cake, how many pieces of cake can you form with 3 straight cuts?

62. You have 7 tennis balls that are all identical but one of them is slightly lighter than the others. Using a balance scale and only two separate weighings, how can you find the light tennis ball?

63. You're going to a friend's house and want to give them some brownies. On the way to their house you cross 5 bridges. At each bridge you must pay a toll of half of your brownies to the owner. But they are all very nice and give you back a brownie from what you give them. How many brownies must you start with to give your friend 2 brownies?

64. Today my car mileage meter reads 72927 kms. I note that this is a palindrome (the same read forwards or backwards). What is the minimum number of kms I need to travel in order for my car meter to register another palindrome?

65. Sue is now four-fifths of her sister Kate's age. Three years ago, she was one-half her sister's age. Five years from now, Sue will be nine-tenths of Kate's age. If they are both under age 10, how old are they now?

66. Bill climbs a 2-mile hill at an uphill speed of 2 MPH, spends no time at the top, and immediately walks down at 6 MPH. What is his average speed for the up and down trip?

67. Can you solve the following sequence:
11, 12, 26, 81, 82, 166, 501, 502, 1006, ?

68. If 3 salesmen can sell three stoves in seven minutes, how many stoves can six salesmen sell in seventy minutes?

69. Dave was paddling his canoe upstream at a constant rate. After six miles, the wind blew his hat into the stream. Thinking that he had no chance to recover his hat, he continued upstream for six more miles before turning back. He continued rowing at the same rate on his return trip and overtook his hat at exactly the same spot where he began his journey eight hours earlier. What was the velocity of the stream?

70. How many different ways can seven people arrange themselves in a row of seven seats?

71. My father is three times as old as my sister, who is twice as old as my brother, who is twice as old as our nephew. The total of all ages is divisible by five and less than 100. How old is my father?

72. A bolt of cloth is colored as follows: one third and one quarter of it are black, the other 8 yards are gray. How long is the bolt?

73. Replace the 'a' letters with mathematical symbols to make the following equation work:
6 a 6 a 66 a 6 a 66 = 113

74. If a crab and a half weigh a pound and a half, but the half crab weighs half as much again as the whole crab. What do half the whole crab and the whole of the half crab weigh?

75. If you had a piece of paper that was 0.0001 meters thick, how tall a pile would it make if it was doubled fifty times?

76. If you reverse the digits of my age, you have the age of my daughter. A year ago, I was twice her age. How old are we both now?

77. You can buy 3 bags of jellybeans and 2 bags of chocolate chips for 24¢. You can also get 4 bags of chocolates and 2 bags of jellybeans for the same 24¢. How much did each bag of chocolates cost?

78. There are 100 people applying for a position where they will be required to sell both music equipment and electronic goods. Twelve of the applicants have no prior experience in sales. Sixty-four of the applicants have sold music equipment, and 80 applicants have sold electronic goods previously. How many applicants have experience selling both music equipment and electronic goods?

79. If a bouquet of six tulips and eight daisies costs $10, but a bouquet of eight tulips and six daisies costs $11, how much does each flower cost?

80. In the farmyard are a number of sheep and hens. There are twice as many hens as sheep, and if you add the total number of heads between them to the total number of legs, you get 187. How many are there of each animal?

81. If you had a pizza with crust thickness 'a' and radius 'z', what's the volume of the pizza?

82. What is the value of 1/2 of 2/3 of 3/4 of 4/5 of 5/6 of 6/7 of 7/8 of 8/9 of 9/10 of 1,000?

83. If you had an infinite supply of water and a 5-liter and 3-liter bucket, how would you measure exactly 4 liters?

84. What would be the next number in the following sequence?
11   1,331   161,051   19,487,171   ?

85. A fish is fifteen inches long. Its head is as long as its tail. If the head were twice as long as it really is, the head and tail would together be as long as what's in between. How long is each part of the fish?

86. If I buy an apple and a banana, the cost will be $1.19. If I buy an apple and a pear, the cost will be $1.45. If I buy a banana and a pear, the cost will be $1.40. What are the individual prices?

87. A box of candy bars can be divided equally (without cutting anything) among 2, 3, or 7 people. What is the least number of candy bars the box could contain?

88. Replace the @ symbols with standard mathematical symbols, like +, -, and x, to make the following equation true:
9 @ 8 @ 7 @ 6 @ 5 @ 4 = 91

89. If Timmy's toy soldiers are set up in rows of 3 across, one is left over; in rows of 4, 2 are left over; in rows of 5, 3 are left over; and in rows of 6, 4 are left over. What's the least number of toy soldiers Timmy could have?

90. A farmer goes to the market with $100 cash. He must buy exactly 100 animals. There are cows, geese and chicken for sale. A cow costs $15, a goose is $1 and a chicken costs $0.25. He must buy at least one of each animal and has to spend all his money. What does the farmer buy?

91. The day before yesterday I was 25 and next year, I will be 28. This is true on only one day in a year. What day is my birthday?

92. Julie says to her brother Pete: "I have as many sisters as brothers." "Yeah, well," replies Pete: "I've got twice as many sisters as I have brothers." How many sisters and brothers are there?

93. Terry is half as old as Alice was when Alice was five years older than Terry is now. How old is Terry now?

94. Two wine merchants arrive at the gates of Paris. One has 64 and the other has 20 barrels of wine. Since they have not enough money to pay the custom duties, the first pays 40 francs and 5 barrels of wine. The second pays 2 barrels of wine but receives 40 francs in change. What is the value of each barrel of wine and what is the duty payable?

95. "How much is this bag of potatoes?" asked the man. "32 lb divided by half its own weight," said the green grocer. How much did the potatoes weigh?

96. How high would you have to count before you used the letter 'a'?

97. When can you add 2 to 11 and get 1?

98. Frank is eight years older than his sister. In three years, he will be twice as old as she will be. How old are they now?

99. I am a number. Add 47 to me. Multiply the sum times 3. Divide the product by 2. You end up with 81. What number am I?

100. Find the smallest +ve mathematical number which is spelled in an alphabetical order.

101. The ages of a father and son add up to 66. The father's age is the son's age reversed. Give three sets of possible ages they could be.

102. King Tut died 120 years after King Eros was born. Their combined ages when they died was 100 years. King Eros died in the year 40 B.C. In what year was King Tut born?

103. Using only addition, how do you add eight 8s and get the number 1,000?

104. A fast food restaurant sells chicken in orders of 6, 9, and 20. What is the largest number of pieces of chicken you cannot order from this restaurant?

105. What number is missing from the following series:
31, 62, 93, 25, 56, ?

106. You are in a roomful of 10 people. Everyone is asked to shake hands with everyone. How many handshakes will there be?

107. A claustrophobic person gets on a train. The train enters a tunnel just as it is leaving the station. Where is the best place for him to sit?

108. Suppose you're on a game show, and you're given the choice of three doors: Behind one door is a sports car; behind all of the others are bicycles. You pick a door, say No. 1, and the host, who knows what's behind the doors, opens another door, say No. 2, revealing a bicycle. He then says to you, "Do you want to pick door No. 3?" Is it to your advantage to switch your choice?

109. What is the next number in the sequence?
    1
    11
    21
    1211
    111221
    312211

110. There are 100 coins scattered in a dark room. 90 have heads facing up and 10 are facing tails up. You cannot tell which coins are which. How do you sort the coins into two piles that contain the same number of tails up coins?

111. If 1 + 9 + 8 = 1, what is 2 + 8 + 9?

112. There is a 100-pound watermelon laying out in the sun. 99 percent of the watermelon's weight is water. After laying out for a few hours 98 percent of the watermelon's weight is water. How much water evaporated?

113. If you have 30 white socks, 22 black socks, and 14 blue socks scattered across the floor in the dark, how many would you have to grab to get a matching pair?

114. If you have an 11-minute and 13-minute hourglass, how can you accurately time 15 minutes?

115. You have found a mutant alga that doubles in size every hour. It takes 18 hours for one algae plant to take up half of a certain lake. How long would it take for two of these plants to take up half of the same lake?

116. You have been given the task of transporting 3,000 apples 1,000 miles from Appleland to Bananaville. Your truck can carry 1,000 apples at a time. Every time you travel a mile towards Bananaville you must pay a tax of 1 apple but you pay nothing when going in the other direction (towards Appleland). What is the highest number of apples you can get to Bananaville?

117. You have 10 bags with 1,000 coins each. In one of the bags, all coins are forgeries. A true coin weighs 1 gram; each counterfeit coin weighs 1.1 gram. If you have an accurate scale, which you can use only once, how can you identify the bag with the forgeries?

118. Can you arrange 9 numerals - 1, 2, 3, 4, 5, 6, 7, 8 and 9 - (using each numeral just once) above and below a division line, to create a fraction equaling to 1/3?

119. Can you arrange four nines to make it equal to 100 using two mathematical symbols?

120. If 1/3 of some number is 1/17 of 1/5, what is that number?

121. The combined ages of Mark and Andrew are 44, and Mark is twice as old as Andrew was when Mark was half as old as Andrew will be when Andrew is three times as old as Mark was when Mark was three times as old as Andrew. How old is Mark?

122. Solve the sequence below:
8, 61, 42, 23, 04, 84, ?

123. What is the missing number in the sequence below?
17, 24, 1, 9, 23, 8, ?, 13, 27, 35, 12, 19

124. In a recent contest, 45 participants were awarded $300,000 in prize money. The money was divided into prizes of $4,000 and $8,000. Each of the participants received one prize. How many participants received the $4,000 prize and how many received the $8,000 amount?

125. What is the next number in the following sequence?
4   8   32   128   2,048   ?

126. Using the numbers 1 through 9, how many three-digit palindromic numbers can you make? A palindrome reads the same forward and backward. Examples: 181, 545, 858.

127. Between which two numbers in the following list should you put the number 4? Why?
8, 50, 19, 1, 17, 6, 10, 13, 30, 20

128. What is the missing number in the sequence below?
361,117   360,204   359,291   358,378
357,465   ?

129. AB + CD + (EF/GH) + (I/J) = 100
Each of the ten digits, from 0 to 9 has been used once and only once in the construction of the above sum. Can you replace the letters with the digits? There is more than one valid answer.

130. How can you make the following equation correct:
8 + 8 = 91

131. Use the numbers 8, 5, 1 and 1 to equal 10 by using mathematical symbols.

132. Solve:

alfa + beta + gamma = delta

133. The following multiplication example uses
every digit from 0 to 9 once (not counting
the intermediate steps). Fill in the missing
numbers:

7 x x
  4 x
x x x x x

134. What is the next number in the following
series:

1, 2, 6, 30, 60, 180, 900, 1800, 5400, ?

135. We know that 5 squared = 25. Can you use
the numbers 2 and 5 once and only once
and any math sign or symbol to arrive at 25
differently?

136. I asked two people to give me their ages.
The did so, and then, to test their
arithmetical powers, I asked each of them to
add the two ages together. One gave me 44
as the answer, and the other gave me 1,280.
I immediately saw that one of them had
subtracted one age from the other, while the
other person had multiplied the two ages
together. Can you tell what their ages were?

137. Can you arrange four 9s, and use at most 2 math symbols, to make the total be 100?

138. Can you get a sum of 1,000 using sixteen 4s and only additions?

139. A farmer challenges an engineer, a physicist, and a mathematician to fence off the largest amount of area using the least amount of fence. The engineer made his fence in a circle and said it was the most efficient. The physicist made a long line and said that the length was infinite. Then he said that fencing half of the Earth was the best. The mathematician laughed at the others and with his design beat the others. What did he do?

140. I have two coins. One of the coins is a faulty coin having a tail on both sides of it. The other coin is a perfect coin (heads on one side and tail on the other). I blindfold myself and pick a coin and put the coin on table. The face of coin towards the sky is tail. What is the probability that other side is also tail?

141. Three men in a cafe order a meal of which the total cost is $15. They each contribute $5. The waiter takes the money to the chef who recognizes the three as friends and asks the waiter to return $5 to the men. The waiter is not only poor at mathematics but dishonest and instead of going to the trouble of splitting the $5 between the three he simply gives them $1 each and pockets the remaining $2 for himself. Now, each of the men effectively paid $4, the total paid is therefore $12. Add the $2 in the waiter's pocket and this comes to $14. So, where has the other $1 gone from the original $15?

142. There was a magic tree that on the first day increased its height by half, on the second day by a third, on the third day by a quarter, and so on. How many days did it take it to grow one hundred times its original height?

143. A girl was eight years old on her first birthday. How could that be?

144. Dave asked his grandma how old she was. She said "I have six children, and there are 4 years between each one and the next. I had my first child at 19. Now the youngest is 19". How old is Dave's grandma?

145. Find a 10-digit number where the first digit is how many 0s in the answer, the second digit is how many 1s in the answer, etc. until the 10th digit is how many 9s in the answer.

146. Three men go fishing on a camping trip. They collect all the fish they caught and put them in a cooler. They agree that when they leave, they will divide up the fish equally. In the middle of the night the first man gets sick and decides to leave. He opens the cooler and counts the fish. He throws one fish away and then takes his third of the fish. Later that night the second man has a family emergency and decides to leave. He opens the cooler and counts the fish. He throws one fish away and then takes his third of the fish. The third man gets up very early the next morning and decides to leave. He opens the cooler and counts the fish. He throws one fish away and then takes his third of the fish. None of the men know that the other men had taken any fish. What is the smallest number of fish that would make this possible?

147. A man walks into a bar, orders a drink, and starts talking to the bartender. During their conversation, the customer learns that the bartender has three children. "How old are your children?" asks the customer. The bartender replies: "The product of their ages is 72." The man thinks for a minute and says: "That's not enough information." The bartender replies: "Okay, if you go outside and look at the building number posted over the door to the bar, you'll see the sum of their ages." The man goes outside, and after a couple of minutes he comes back in and tells the bartender: "That is still not enough information." The bartender smiles and says: "My youngest just loves strawberry ice cream." The customer thinks for a few more minutes and finally says: "Now I know how old they are." How old are the children?

148. A freight train leaves Unionville at 6:00 pm and is traveling towards Stonesboro at 15 MPH. A passenger train leaves Stonesboro at 6:00 pm and is traveling towards Unionville at 85 MPH. Unionville and Stonesboro are 200 miles apart. When and where will the two trains meet?

149. The population of Orangedale is 4,800 more than Troutville. If 3,100 people move from Troutville to Orangedale, the population of Orangedale will be eleven times the population of Troutville. Find the original population of Orangedale and Troutville.

150. By using the numbers 7, 3, 7, 3 and with any math signs can you make them add up to 24?

DIFFICULT RIDDLES ANSWERS

1. *ONE OF THE 'FATHERS' IS ALSO A GRANDFATHER. THEREFORE, THE OTHER FATHER IS BOTH A SON AND A FATHER TO THE GRANDSON. IN OTHER WORDS, THE ONE FATHER IS BOTH A SON AND A FATHER.*

2. *25. THE NUMBERS ARE THE SQUARES OF 1, 2, 3, 4, 5, 6, AND 7*

3. *9 & 1. THERE ARE TWO SERIES, ONE STARTING WITH 10 AND GOING DOWN ONE NUMBER EACH TIME, AND ONE STARTING WITH 1 AND GOING UP ONE NUMBER EACH TIME.*

4. *44 AND 66*

5. *ONCE, AFTER THAT YOU ARE SUBTRACTING IT FROM 20.*

6. *194*

7. *1, 2 & 3*

8. *4 CHILDREN GET 1 APPLE EACH WHILE THE FIFTH CHILD GETS THE BASKET WITH THE REMAINING APPLE STILL IN IT.*

9. *20*

10. *50%*

11. *20 TIMES. (8, 18, 28, 38, 48, 58, 68, 78, 80, 81, 82, 83, 84, 85, 86, 87, 88, 89, 98).*

12. *95. DIVIDING BY 1/2 IS THE SAME AS MULTIPLYING BY 2. SO, 40 X 2 + 15 = 95.*

13. *JOHN WINS AGAIN. IN THE FIRST RACE JOHN RAN 100 METERS IN THE TIME IT TOOK PETER TO RUN 95 METERS. SO, IN THE SECOND RACE WHEN PETER IS AT THE 95 METER MARK, JOHN WILL ALSO BE THERE (SINCE 100 - 5 = 95). SINCE JOHN IS FASTER, HE WILL PASS PETER IN THE LAST 5 METERS OF THE RACE.*

14. *HE LOST $5. THE LADY FROM THE FLOWER SHOP GAVE HIM $20 IN CHANGE, BUT EVENTUALLY GOT $20 BACK. SHE BROKE EVEN. THE MAN WHO GOT THE HAIRCUT GAVE THE BARBER NOTHING (EXCEPT COUNTERFEIT MONEY) BUT GOT $5 BACK FROM THE BARBER. SO, THE BARBER LOST ONLY $5, AND GAVE A FREE HAIRCUT.*

15. *THEY WILL BE THE SAME DISTANCE AWAY WHEN THEY MEET.*

16. *Two twins are 2 people, three triplets are 3 people, and four quadruplets are 4 people. Therefore 2 + 3 + 4 = 9.*

17. *When the test began, the teacher turned both 7-min and 11-min hourglasses. After the 7-min one spilt its last grain, he turned it upside down (the 11-min one is still to spill sand for another 4 minutes). When the 11-min hourglass was spilt, he turned the 7-min one upside down for the last time.*

18. *A decimal point. 5.9*

19. *6,666*

20. *46. Add 2 and the difference between the previous numbers to the last number.*

21. *Twenty people split a $600 dollar bill.*

22. *6.25*

23. *It takes a puzzle solver 6 minutes to solve a puzzle. Therefore, to solve 60 puzzles it takes 360 minutes, or 6 hours.*

24. *30 AND 195. THINK OF IT LIKE THIS: IF THERE IS A RATIO OF 2 TO 13, THEN THERE ARE 15 TOTAL PARTS (2 + 13). ONE FIFTEENTH OF 225 IS 15 OR ONE PART. TWO PARTS ARE 2 X 15 OR 30, LEAVING 13 PARTS X 15 OR 195. 30/195 = 2/13.*

25. *6,413*

26. *IF THE LENGTH OF THE ROPE + 2 YARDS = 3 TIMES THE LENGTH OF THE ROPE, THEN THE ROPE IS 1 YARD LONG.*

27. *10 (1000 ÷ 4 = 250 ÷ 10 = 25 ÷ 5 = 5 + 5 = 10).*

28. *3*

29. *24 AND 60*

30. *THERE IS A TOTAL OF 10 MATCHES. AFTER EVERY MATCH, 2 POINTS WERE DISTRIBUTED BETWEEN TWO TEAMS. THEREFORE 10 X 2 = 20 POINTS IS THE SUM OF ALL THE TEAMS' POINTS.*
6 + 5 + 4 + 2 + ? =20
? = 3

31. *15¢. THE COST IS EQUAL TO 3¢ FOR EACH LETTER IN THE FRUIT'S NAME.*

32. *47 + 53 + 59 + 61 = 220*

33. *1*

34. *104 AND 96. THERE ARE REALLY 2 SERIES IN ONE, ONE STARTS AT 101 AND COUNTS UP; THE OTHER STARTS AT 99 AND COUNTS DOWN.*

35. *KEVIN FLEW AT 666.67 MILES PER HOUR OVER HIS ENTIRE TRIP.*

36. *5*

37. *SHE HAD FIVE WRONG ANSWERS. IF ANNETTE HAD ANSWERED ALL 20 QUESTIONS CORRECTLY, SHE WOULD HAVE SCORED 200. SINCE SHE ONLY SCORED 125, SHE MUST HAVE LOST 75 POINTS. SINCE EACH INCORRECT ANSWER RESULTS IN A TOTAL LOSS OF 15 POINTS (10 FOR NOT GETTING IT CORRECT AND 5 FOR ANSWERING INCORRECTLY) SHE MUST HAVE MISSED 5 QUESTIONS. 5 x 15 = 75, 200 - 75 = 125.*

38. *LET R = THE NUMBER OF RABBITS AND C = THE NUMBER OF CHICKENS. THEN, R + C = 72. 4R + 2C = 200. TO SOLVE, WE MULTIPLY THE FIRST EQUATION BY 2, AND THEN SUBTRACT IT FROM THE SECOND EQUATION.*
$$4R + 2C = 200 \; (\text{-}) \; R + 2C = 144,$$
THUS $2R = 56 = R = 28$, $C = 44$. *SO, THERE ARE* 28 *RABBITS AND* 44 *CHICKENS.*

39. *THE MAXIMUM IS* 63.

40. *SINCE EACH ASSISTANT TAKES* 1.5 *HOURS PER BOX, IT WILL TAKE AN HOUR AND A HALF.*

41. 40 *MILES APART*

42. $X + 2 = 2(X - 5)$
$X + 2 = 2X - 10$
$X = 12$

43. 6

44. $18 \& 81$

45. 1 *OUT OF* 8. *THERE ARE* 16 *COMBINATIONS THAT COULD EXIST, BUT ONLY TWO ARE EITHER ALL GIRLS OR ALL BOYS.*

46. *5 CATS. THE SAME FIVE COULD KEEP CATCHING 5 MICE EVERY 5 MINUTES FOR 100 MINUTES.*

47. *8 MEN AND 14 HORSES.*
     LET M = MEN AND H = HORSES. WE CAN COME UP WITH 2 EQUATIONS:
     M + H = 22
     2M + 4H= 72

48. *FOR THE TRAIN TO PASS COMPLETELY THROUGH THE TUNNEL, IT MUST TRAVEL 2 MILES.*
     AFTER 1 MILE OF TRAVEL, THE TRAIN WOULD BE COMPLETELY IN THE TUNNEL, AND AFTER ANOTHER MILE IT WOULD BE COMPLETELY OUT AND SINCE THE TRAIN IS TRAVELING AT 1 MILE A MINUTE, IT WILL TAKE 2 MINUTES TO PASS THROUGH THE TUNNEL.

49. *1.5*

50. *3 WATERMELONS*

FIENDISH RIDDLES ANSWERS

51. *BLUE BALLS = 15, RED BALLS = 36 & GREEN BALLS = 9*

52. *HE HAD 6 ORANGES TO START WITH, AND ATE 2 THE FIRST DAY AND 2 THE SECOND DAY.*

53. *41 YEARS AGO, WHEN SALLY WAS 13 AND HER MOTHER WAS 39.*

54. *TIP THE GLASS OF WATER UNTIL THE WATER REACHES THE RIM OF THE GLASS AND IF THE WATER LINES UP PERFECTLY WITH THE BOTTOM RIM OF THE GLASS, IT IS HALF FULL.*

55. *THE TIDE RAISES BOTH THE WATER AND THE BOAT SO THE WATER WILL NEVER REACH THE FIFTH RUNG.*

56. *0. ALL NUMBERS MULTIPLIED BY 0 ARE 0.*

57. *9*

58. *THE MINUTE HAND IS POINTING DIRECTLY AT THE '3'. THE HOUR HAND IS 1/4 OF THE WAY BETWEEN THE '3' AND '4'. SINCE THERE ARE 12 NUMBERS, THE ANGLE BETWEEN EACH NUMBER IS 30 DEGREES. SO, THE ANGLE BETWEEN THE HANDS ARE 30 DEGREES * 1/4 = 7.5 DEGREES.*

59. *Start one of the ropes on fire from both ends and the other one from one end. After half an hour one rope will be completely burnt and the other will be half burnt. At this point you light the final rope from the unlit side and it will take 15 minutes for the remaining half of the rope to burn, for a total of 45 minutes.*

60. *$56.25.*
    25% off $100 is $75. Now the second 25% is taken off the sales price, so 25% of $75 is $18.75. Subtract that from $75 and you get $56.25.

61. *8 pieces. Make two cuts like you normally would then one horizontal cut from the side of the cake.*

62. *Put three of the balls on each side. If they are even the ball that wasn't weighed is the light one. If they aren't even the side that is lighter has the light ball. Of these three balls, one should be put on each side. If the sides are even then the other ball is the light one. If they aren't even the one that is lighter is the ball you're looking for.*

63. *JUST 2. EACH TIME YOU GIVE THE OWNER OF A BRIDGE HALF OF YOUR BROWNIES (1 BROWNIE) THEY GIVE YOU ONE BACK AS WELL.*

64. *110 KMS SO THAT THE TOTAL IS 73037.*

65. *SUE IS 4 AND KATE IS 5.*

66. *3 MPH. IT TAKES 1 HOUR TO GO UP THE HILL AND 20 MINUTES TO GO DOWN. THAT IS 80 MINUTES FOR 4 MILES WHICH IS 20 MINUTES PER MILE OR 3 MPH.*

67. *3021.*
   THE SEQUENCE IS TO MULTIPLY BY 1 & THEN ADD 1, MULTIPLY BY 2 & THEN ADD 2, MULTIPLY BY 3 & ADD 3, MULTIPLY BY 1 & ADD 1, MULTIPLY BY 2 & ADD 2, MULTIPLY BY 3 & ADD 3, ETC.

68. *SIX SALESMEN CAN SELL 60 STOVES IN SEVENTY MINUTES.*

69. *1 MPH. Dave was rowing at a constant rate in relation to the water, and it took him eight hours to travel 24 miles. At the point where he lost his hat, he had been rowing for six miles, or two hours. To meet Dave where he began his journey, the hat had to travel downstream six miles. Dave didn't reach the hat until after he had rowed the remaining 18 miles, or for six more hours. Thus, it took the hat six hours to travel six miles, carried by the stream velocity of 1 MPH.*

70. *5,040 ways.*
   7 x 6 x 5 x 4 x 3 x 2 x 1. The first person can choose any of 7 seats, the second person any of 6 seats, the third any of five seats, etc.

71. *60. Here is how to get it:*
   Nephew = x, brother = 2x, sister = 4x, father = 12x, total of 19x = some number divisible by 5 but less than 100. The only number that fits is 95; so 19x = 95 and therefore x = 5. Nephew = 5, brother = 10, sister = 20 and father = 60.

72. *19.2 yards.*

73. *6 x 6 + 66/6 + 66 = 113.*

74. *2.1 POUNDS. THE WHOLE CRAB MUST WEIGH 0.6 POUNDS, AND THE HALF CRAB 0.9 POUNDS, TOTALING 1 1/2 POUNDS. IF THE FORMER WERE HALVED AND THE LATTER DOUBLED, THE WEIGHTS WOULD THEN BE 0.3 AND 1.8 POUNDS, TOTALING 2.1 POUNDS.*

75. *112,589,991 KILOMETERS*

76. *MY DAUGHTER IS 37 AND I AM 73.*

77. *EACH BAG OF CHOCOLATES COSTS 3¢.*

78. *56. SINCE 12 APPLICANTS HAVE HAD NO SALES EXPERIENCE, THERE ARE 88 APPLICANTS WHO HAVE SOME EXPERIENCE IN SALES. OF THE 88 APPLICANTS, 64 HAVE SOLD MUSIC EQUIPMENT, WHICH LEAVES 24 WHO HAVE NOT. EIGHTY APPLICANTS HAVE SOLD ELECTRONIC GOODS, WHICH LEAVES 8 WHO HAVE NOT. IN OTHER WORDS, 32 APPLICANTS (24+8) COULD NOT HAVE SOLD BOTH AND 56 APPLICANTS (88-32) HAVE SOLD BOTH.*

79. *EACH TULIP COSTS $1 AND EACH DAISY COSTS 50¢.*

80. *17 SHEEP AND 34 HENS.*

81. *PI * z * z *A*

82. *100. JUST WORK IT BACKWARDS AND YOU'LL FIND IT VERY EASY.*

83. *FILL THE 5-LITER BUCKET FIRST. THEN USING THAT BUCKET FILL THE 3-LITER BUCKET BEING CAREFUL NOT TO SPILL ANY. THIS LEAVES 2 LITERS IN THE 5-LITER BUCKET. NOW THROW AWAY THE WATER IN THE 3-LITER BUCKET AND REFILL WITH THE REMAINING CONTENTS OF THE BIGGER BUCKET. ONCE AGAIN FILL THE 5-LITER BUCKET AND FILL THE SECOND 3-LITER BUCKET. THIS WILL LEAVE YOU 4 LITERS IN THE 5-LITER BUCKET.*

84. *2,357,947,691.*

    THE NUMBERS ARE 11 TO THE FIRST POWER, 11 TO THE THIRD POWER, 11 TO THE FIFTH POWER, 11 TO THE SEVENTH POWER. THEREFORE, THE MISSING NUMBER IS 11 TO THE NINTH POWER.

85. *THE HEAD AND TAIL ARE EACH THREE INCHES LONG; THE REST IS NINE.*

86. *PEAR = 83¢, BANANA = 57¢, APPLE = 62¢.*

87. *THE LOWEST COMMON DENOMINATOR OF 2, 3, AND 7 IS 2 X 3 X 7 OR 42.*

88. 9 x 8 - 7 + 6 x 5 - 4 = 91

89. 58

90. 3 COWS, 41 GEESE AND 56 CHICKENS

*91. HIS BIRTHDAY IS ON DECEMBER 31.
HE MADE THE STATEMENT ON JANUARY 1. ON THE DAY
BEFORE YESTERDAY (DECEMBER 30) HE WAS 25. HE
TURNED 26 ON DECEMBER 31. THAT YEAR, HE WOULD
TURN 27, SO THE "NEXT YEAR" HE WOULD TURN 28.*

*92. THERE ARE 4 SISTERS AND 3 BROTHERS. JULIE HAS 3
SISTERS AND 3 BROTHERS, AND PETE HAS 2 BROTHERS
AND 4 SISTERS.*

93. TERRY IS 5 YEARS OLD. LET'S TRANSLATE WORDS TO MATH:

    "ALICE WAS FIVE YEARS OLDER THAN TERRY IS NOW" TRANSLATES TO: $A = 5 + T$, WHERE A IS THE AGE OF ALICE AND T IS THE AGE OF TERRY.

    NOW TRANSLATE AGAIN. "TERRY IS HALF AS OLD AS ALICE WAS" BECOMES: $T = (1/2)A$. SOLVING THE TWO EQUATIONS WILL GIVE $T = 5$.

94. THE VALUE OF A BARREL IS 120 FRANCS AND THE DUTY IS 10 FRANCS A BARREL.

95. 8 LBS.

96. ONE THOUSAND

97. WHEN YOU ARE TALKING OF A CLOCK. 2 HOURS TO 11 O'CLOCK MAKE 1 O'CLOCK.

98. FRANK IS *13* AND HIS SISTER IS *5*.

LET *f* REPRESENT FRANK'S AGE.

LET *s* REPRESENT HIS SISTER'S AGE.

FRANK IS EIGHT YEARS OLDER THAN HIS SISTER.

SO $f = s + 8$.

IN THREE YEARS, FRANK WILL BE TWICE AS OLD AS HIS SISTER WILL BE.

SO $f + 3 = 2(s + 3)$.

NOW SUBSTITUTE THE VALUE OF *f* INTO THE EQUATION AND SOLVE FOR *s*.

$s + 8 + 3 = 2(s + 3)$

$s + 11 = 2s + 6$

$11 = s + 6$

$5 = s$.

SINCE THE SISTER'S AGE IS *5* THEN FRANK'S AGE IS *13*.

99. *I AM 7.*

    LET N REPRESENT THE NUMBER.

    ADD 47 TO ME: 47 + N.

    MULTIPLY THE SUM BY 3: (47 + N)3

    DIVIDE THE PRODUCT BY 2: ((47 + N)3) / 2

    YOU END UP WITH 81.

    ((47 + N)3) / 2 = 81

    (47 + N)3 = 162

    47 + N = 54

    N = 7

100. *40*

101. 51 AND 15, 42 AND 24 & 60 AND 06

102. KING TUT WAS BORN IN 20 B.C. THERE WERE 120 YEARS BETWEEN THE BIRTH OF KING EROS AND THE DEATH OF KING TUT, BUT SINCE THEIR AGES AMOUNTED TO ONLY 100 YEARS, THERE MUST HAVE BEEN 20 YEARS WHEN NEITHER EXISTED. THIS WOULD BE A PERIOD BETWEEN THE DEATH OF KING EROS, 40 B.C., AND THE BIRTH OF KING TUT, 20 B.C.

103. 888 + 88 + 8 + 8 + 8 = 1000

104. 43.

*AFTER 6 ALL NUMBERS DIVISIBLE BY 3 CAN BE ORDERED (BECAUSE THEY CAN ALL BE EXPRESSED AS A SUM OF 6S AND 9S). AFTER 26, ALL NUMBERS DIVISIBLE BY THREE WHEN SUBTRACTED BY 20 CAN BE OBTAINED. AFTER 46, ALL NUMBERS DIVISIBLE BY THREE WHEN SUBTRACTED BY 40 CAN BE OBTAINED. AFTER 46, ALL NUMBERS FIT INTO ONE OF THESE 3 CATEGORIES, SO ALL NUMBERS CAN BE OBTAINED. 43 IS THE LAST NUMBER THAT DOESN'T FALL INTO ONE OF THESE CATEGORIES (44 = 20 + 6 X 4, 45 = 6 * 6 + 9).*

105. 87. THESE ARE MULTIPLES OF 13 WITH REVERSE DIGITS: 13, 26, 39, 52, 65, 78.

106. 9+8+7+6+5+4+3+2+1 = 45

FIRST PERSON MUST SHAKE 9 OTHER PEOPLE'S HAND TO HAVE SHAKEN EVERYBODY'S, THE SECOND PERSON HAS ALREADY SHAKEN 1 SO HE HAS TO SHAKE 8 MORE, AND SO ON UNTIL EVERYONE HAS SHAKEN EACH OTHER'S HAND.

107. IN THE BACK. THE TRAIN WILL BE ACCELERATING SO IT WILL BE GOING FASTER WHEN THE BACK OF THE TRAIN ENTERS THE TUNNEL. THEREFORE, A PERSON IN THE BACK WILL SPEND LESS TIME IN THE TUNNEL.

108. YES, BY CHANGING YOUR ANSWER YOUR CHANCES OF WINNING ACTUALLY GOES UP FROM 1/3 TO 2/3.

109. THE NEXT NUMBER IS 13112221. EACH NUMBER DESCRIBES THE PREVIOUS NUMBER. STARTING WITH 1, THE SECOND LINE DESCRIBES IT 11 (ONE 1). THEN THE THIRD LINE DESCRIBES 11 AS 21 (TWO 1S). THEN THE FOURTH LINE DESCRIBES 21 AS 1211 (ONE 2, ONE 1). THIS IS THE PATTERN.

110. The piles don't need to be the same size, so make a pile of 10 coins and a pile of 90 coins, flip all of the ten coins and it is guaranteed that the piles have the same number of tails.

111. 10. Take the first letter of each spelled out number.

112. 50%. In the beginning, it is 99 pounds water and 1 pound other stuff. At the end, the 1 pound other stuff is 2 percent, so the total weight is 50 pounds.
50 pounds - 1 pound other stuff = 49 pounds water. So, 99 pounds - 49 pounds = 50 pounds water lost.

113. Once you grab 4 you will have 2 of the same color.

114. Start both hourglasses. Then when the 11-minute hourglass has finished, immediately flip it again. When the 13-minute hourglass runs out, the 11-minute hourglass will have 9 minutes left, so flip it and it will last another 2 minutes.
13 minutes + 2 minutes = 15 minutes.

115. *17 HOURS. AT 17 HOURS THE ONE PLANT WILL TAKE UP 1/4 OF THE LAKE (1/2 OF 1/2). AT 17 HOURS THE TWO PLANTS WOULD BE DOUBLE THE SIZE OF THE ONE PLANT AND DOUBLE 1/4 IS ONE HALF.*

116. *833 APPLES.*

STEP ONE: FIRST YOU WANT TO MAKE 3 TRIPS OF 1,000 APPLES 333 MILES. YOU WILL BE LEFT WITH 2,001 APPLES AND 667 MILES TO GO.

STEP TWO: NEXT YOU WANT TO TAKE 2 TRIPS OF 1,000 APPLES 500 MILES. YOU WILL BE LEFT WITH 1,000 APPLES AND 167 MILES TO GO (YOU HAVE TO LEAVE AN APPLE BEHIND).

STEP THREE: FINALLY, YOU TRAVEL THE LAST 167 MILES WITH ONE LOAD OF 1,000 APPLES AND ARE LEFT WITH 833 APPLES IN BANANAVILLE.

117. *IF THERE IS ONLY 1 BAG WITH FORGERIES, THEN TAKE 1 COIN FROM THE FIRST BAG, 2 COINS FROM THE SECOND BAG ... TEN COINS FROM THE TENTH BAG AND WEIGH THE PICKED COINS. FIND OUT HOW MANY GRAMS IT WEIGHS AND COMPARE IT TO THE IDEAL STATE OF HAVING ALL ORIGINAL COINS. THE AMOUNT OF GRAMS (THE DIFFERENCE) IS THE PLACE OF THE BAG WITH FAKE COINS.*

118. 5832/17496 = 1/3

119. 99 + 9/9=100

120. 3/85.
   1/3x = 1/17 x 1/5
   1/3x = 1/85
   x = 3/85

121. MARK IS 27 AND 1/2 AND ANDREW IS 16 AND 1/2.

122. 65. THESE ARE MULTIPLES OF 8 WITH THE DIGITS REVERSED.

123. STARTING WITH THE FIRST NUMBER 17, AND THE LAST NUMBER, 19, AND WORKING TOWARDS THE MIDDLE, EACH PAIR TOTALS 36.

124. Let's say A = participants receiving $4,000 in prize money and B = participants receiving $8,000 in prize money. $A + B = 45$.

$4,000(A) + 8,000(B) = 300,000$, substituting:

$4,000 (45-B) + 8,000(B) = 300,000$,

$180,000 - 4,000(B) = 300,000$,

$180,000 - 4,000(B) + 8,000(B) = 300,000$,

$4,000(B) = 120,000 (B) = 30$.

So, 15 people each received $4,000 and 30 people received $8,000.

125. 8,192 or 2 to the 13th power. The sequence is built on the number 2 being raised to the consecutive prime numbers.

2 to the 2nd power = 4; 2 to the 3rd power = 8; 2 to the 5th power = 32; 2 to the 7th power = 128; etc.

126. 81 palindrome numbers can be made.

127. Between 50 and 19. When spelled out, the numbers appear in alphabetical order.

128. 356,552. Each succeeding number is 913 less than its predecessor.

129. $17 + 82 + (45/90) + (3/6) = 100$

130. *Turn it upside down so that*

$16 = 8 + 8$

131. $8/ (1 - 1/5)$

132. $5795 + 6435 + 2505 = 14735$ *or*

$5305 + 2475 + 6595 = 14375$

133.   715
          46
      32890

134. *27,000. The repeating pattern is, 2, 3, and 5 times the preceding number.*

135. *Here is one way:* $5 \div .2 = 25.$

136. *The ages were 20 and 64.*

137. $99 / .99$

138. $444 + 444 + 44 + 44 + 4 + 4 + 4 + 4 + 4 + 4 = 1,000$

139. THE MATHEMATICIAN MADE A SMALL FENCE AROUND HIMSELF AND DECLARED HIMSELF TO BE ON THE OUTSIDE.

140. 2/3

POSSIBLE SCENARIOS ARE:

1 A1 (H) A2 (H)

2 A2 (H) A1 (H)

3 B1 (H) B2 (T)

4 B2 (T) B1 (H)

CASE 4 IS NOT POSSIBLE, SO THE ANSWER IS 2/3.

141. *THE PROBLEM IS THAT THE QUESTION IS CLEVERLY PHRASED TO CONCEAL WHAT IS REALLY GOING ON. LET'S LOCATE ALL THAT MONEY. THERE ARE TWO WAYS TO THINK ABOUT HOW MUCH MONEY IS OUT THERE TO BE FOUND. THE WAY THAT THIS QUESTION IS TRICKY IS THAT IT COMBINES THESE TWO WAYS.*

THE FIRST WAY IS THIS: HOW MUCH MONEY DID THE THREE MEN PAY ORIGINALLY.

THE SECOND WAY IS THIS: HOW MUCH MONEY DID THEY END UP PAYING?

SO, IF IT IS THE FIRST WAY, THEN CLEARLY THE TOTAL WE NEED TO ACCOUNT FOR IS THE $15.

THEREFORE, LET'S SEE WHAT HAPPENS TO THAT $15. THE CHEF GETS $10, THE WAITER GETS $2 AND THE GUYS GET $3 BACK. THAT ADDS UP FINE.

NOW, LET'S LOOK AT THE SECOND WAY. HOW MUCH MONEY DID THEY END UP PAYING? WELL $12; $10 OF IT WENT TO THE CHEF AND $2 TO THE WAITER. NOW, THAT ADDS UP TOO.

THE PROBLEM WITH THE QUESTION IS THAT THE $2 THAT THE WAITER TOOK IS CONTAINED IN THE $12 THAT THEY END UP PAYING SO WE SHOULDN'T EXPECT THEM TO ADD TO ANYTHING MEANINGFUL.

142. It will take 198 days. Let's say the tree was originally one foot tall. On the first day, it grew half a foot; on the next day 1/3 of 1.5 feet, which is half a foot, and so on – it grew half a foot every day. So, in 198 days, it grew 99 feet, and then was 100 feet tall.

143. She was born on February 29, 1896. The year 1900 was not a leap year (only centuries divisible by 400 are leap years), so the next February 29 fell in 1904 when she was eight. She was twelve on her second birthday.

144. She is 58 years old.

1st child was born when she was 19.
2nd child was born when she was 23 (19 + 4)
3rd child was born when she was 27 (23 + 4)
4th child was born when she was 31 (27 + 4)
5th child was born when she was 35 (31 + 4)
6th child was born when she was 39 (35 + 4)
The sixth child is 19, so grandma is 58.

145. 6210001000

146. *THE ANSWER IS 25 FISH.*

EACH MAN THROWS AWAY A FISH BEFORE HE TAKES HIS THIRD OF THE TOTAL. SO THE AMOUNT OF FISH IN THE COOLER MUST BE DIVISIBLE BY 3 AFTER ONE FISH IS THROWN AWAY.

THE FIRST MAN SEES 25 FISH. HE THROWS AWAY ONE FISH LEAVING 24 FISH. HE THEN TAKES 8 FISH (24/3) AND THAT LEAVES 16 FISH.

THE SECOND MAN SEES 16 FISH. HE THROWS AWAY ONE FISH LEAVING 15 FISH. HE THEN TAKES 5 FISH (15/3) AND THAT LEAVES 10 FISH.

THE THIRD MAN SEES 10 FISH. HE THROWS AWAY ONE FISH LEAVING 9 FISH. HE THEN TAKES 3 FISH (9/3).

IF YOU TRY THE OTHER NUMBERS SMALLER THAN 25 (22, 19, 16, 13, 10, 7, AND 4) THAT ARE DIVISIBLE BY 3 AFTER THROWING AWAY ONE FISH YOU WILL SEE THEY DO NOT SOLVE THE PROBLEM.

147. *THE ANSWER IS 6 YEARS OLD, 6 YEARS OLD, AND 2 YEARS OLD.*

TO DETERMINE THE ANSWER THE FIRST STEP IS TO PRODUCE ALL THE COMBINATIONS OF THREE AGES THAT CAN BE MULTIPLIED TOGETHER TO GET 72. LISTED BELOW ARE THOSE COMBINATIONS.

72	1	1	18	2	2	9	8	1
36	2	1	12	6	1	8	3	3
24	3	1	12	3	2	6	6	2
18	4	1	9	4	2	6	4	3

THE SECOND STEP IS TO FIND THE SUM OF THESE COMBINATIONS. SINCE THE CUSTOMER SAID KNOWING THE SUM OF THE AGES WAS STILL NOT ENOUGH INFORMATION THEN THERE MUST BE MORE THAN ONE COMBINATION THAT PRODUCES THE SAME SUM. THE COMBINATIONS 8, 3, 3 AND 6, 6, 2 BOTH PRODUCE THE SUM OF 14.

THE LAST STEP USES THE FACT THAT THE BARTENDER MENTIONED HIS YOUNGEST CHILD. THAT MEANS THE CUSTOMER KNOWS ONE CHILD IS YOUNGER THAN THE OTHER TWO. THE CUSTOMER CAN'T FIGURE THAT OUT WITH THE 8, 3, 3 COMBINATION SINCE THERE ARE TWO CHILDREN WITH AN AGE OF 3. THEREFORE, THE AGES OF THE CHILDREN MUST BE THE LAST COMBINATION OF 6, 6, AND 2.

148. *THERE ARE TWO TRAINS TRAVELING TOWARDS EACH OTHER. THE FREIGHT TRAIN IS GOING 15 MPH AND THE PASSENGER TRAIN IS GOING 85 MPH. THEIR TOTAL SPEED, RELATIVE TO EACH OTHER, IS 15 MPH + 85 MPH = 100 MPH.*

USE THE FORMULA DISTANCE = RATE X TIME TO SOLVE THE PROBLEM. THE DISTANCE IS 200 MILES AND THE RATE IS 100 MPH. LET T BE THE TIME THE TWO TRAINS TRAVEL.

NOW WE HAVE 200 MILES = (100 MPH)T.

SO T = 200 MILES / 100 MPH. T=2 HOURS.

THE TRAINS MEET AT 8:00 PM.

USING THE SAME FORMULA (DISTANCE = RATE X TIME) WE CAN NOW DETERMINE HOW FAR EACH TRAIN TRAVELED.

FREIGHT TRAIN: D = (15 MPH) (2 HOURS).

D=30 MILES.

PASSENGER TRAIN: D = (85 MPH) (2 HOURS).

D=170 MILES.

THE TRAINS MEET AT GREENVILLE, WHICH IS 30 MILES FROM UNIONVILLE AND 170 MILES FROM STONESBORO.

149. *Let x = original population of Troutville.*

Let x + 4,800 = original population of Orangedale.

Now 3,100 people move from Troutville to Orangedale.

The new population of Troutville = x – 3100

The new population of Orangedale = x + 4800 + 3100

Now the new population of Orangedale is eleven times the new population of Troutville.

So now we have:

$x + 4800 + 3100 = 11(x - 3100)$

$x + 7900 = 11x - 34100$

$7900 = 10x - 34100$

$42000 = 10x$

$4200 = x$

Original population of Troutville was 4,200.

Original population of Orangedale was 9,000.

150. $7 \times ((3 / 7) + 3) = 24$

One Last Thing

If you have enjoyed this book, I would love you to write a review of it on Amazon. It is really useful feedback as well as untold encouragement to the author.

Any remarks are highly appreciated, so if you have any comments, or suggestions for improvements to this publication, or for other books, I would love to hear from you.

You can contact me at
m.prefontaine2@gmail.com

All your input is greatly valued, and the books have already been revised and improved as a result of helpful suggestions from readers.

Thank you.

Made in the USA
Middletown, DE
14 September 2020